# purpurāria

## a Latin Novella
## by Lance Piantaggini

Poētulus Publishing
magisterp.com

# Index Capitulōrum
# (et Cētera)

# Praefātiō

For this novella, I've gone back to my roots of writing Latin that students can read within the first months. A new character, Poenica, joins the Pisoverse in this tale of 16 cognates and 19 other Latin words (*excluding different forms of the same word, names, and meaning established within the text*), and over 1600 total words in length. The Pisoverse novellas now provide nearly 54,000 total words for the beginning Latin student to read! That's with a vocabulary of just 780 unique words.

Although a low unique word count in texts isn't everything, it's certainly most things when it comes to the beginning student reading Latin. *Poenica purpurāria* is the latest novella with sheltered (i.e. limited) vocabulary available to beginning Latin students.

With fewer word meanings, *Poenica purpurāria* can unshelter (i.e. unleash) its grammar. That is, students are exposed to important and frequent grammar that's typically delayed months or even years in textbook curricula. In this novella, there are a significant number of indirect statements, along with many examples of passive voice, gerundives of purpose, perfect and future tenses, ablative absolute, and the future periphrastic.

One goal of the Pisoverse novellas is to familiarize students with the otherwise unfamiliar distant past through simple descriptions and references. Each book can provide surface level recognition and understanding of antiquity and beyond, or can be used to explore topics further, and more closely. *Poenica purpurāria* can serve as an introduction to quite a variety of topics for a book of its small scope, including the process of dyeing clothes itself, multicultural Rome, women in antiquity, Phoenicians, trade, not to mention Vestals and the broad topic of religion. Teachers are encouraged to make note of what students find compelling, and consider exploring more of that in class.

I'd like to thank all the Pisoverse readers requesting more texts for first year Latin students; there could never be too many of these! I'd also like to thank the Patricias—Pat proper and Christa Patricia—for suggesting a few word changers to make the text clearer.

Aside from a couple older illustrations by me and Lauren Aczon, Chloe Deeley has provided all new illustrations. See more of Chloe's artwork on Instagram @hatchbuddy.

**Magister P**[iantaggini]
Northampton, MA
September 29th, 2020

# I
# Poenica

Poenica purpurāria[1] est.
Poenicae placent colōrēs.

---

[1] **purpurāria** *a purple-dyer. Also, "Poenica" is another word for a Phoenician, people widely known for their purple. So, "Poenica purpurāria" can mean "the purple person who purples!"*

Poenicae multī colōrēs placent.
sed, Poenicae colōrēs purpureī
valdē placent.

colōrēs purpureī extraōrdināriī sunt.
colōrēs purpureī sunt vīvidī—nōn—
vīviDISSIMĪ!

Poenica togās purpurat.
Poenica togās
excellenter purpurat.
Rōmānīs valdē placent
colōrēs purpureī.

Rōmānī volunt togās purpureās.

sed, colōrēs purpureī pretiōsī sunt.
multī Rōmānī purpureās togās
nōn gerunt.


Poenica est purpurāria extraōrdināria.
Poenica est caeca
(i.e. Poenica nōn potest vidēre).
Poenica vidēre nōn potest.
sed, Poenica purpurāria excellēns est.


Poenica est purpurāria excellēns
et extraōrdināria.


sed, Poenica vult esse fūnambula![2]

---

[2] **fūnambula** *tightrope walker*
(**fūnis + ambulāre**) *rope + walk*

# II
# Rūfus in tabernā

Poenica tabernam habet.
taberna Poenicae est Rōmae.[1]


taberna Rōmae est.
sed, Poenica Rōmāna nōn est.

---

[1] **est Rōmae** *is in Rome*

Poenica purpurāria Tyria[2] est.

in tabernā Poenicae,
sunt togae purpureae.
Poenica multās togās purpurat.

sed, Poenica vult esse fūnambula.
Poenica vult esse
fūnambula extraōrdināria.

in tabernā, Poenica fūnem habet.
Poenica vult ambulāre in fūnem.

---

[2] **Tyria** *Tyrian, from Tyre (i.e. Labanon), the Phoenician city. Phoenician lands were known for their purple. Therefore, "Poenica purpurāria Tyria" can mean "the purple-land purple person who purples!"*

subitō, Rūfus
in tabernam Poenicae
ambulat!

Rūfō in tabernā,[3]
Poenica nōn ambulat in fūnem.
Rūfus Poenicam videt.

*Rūfus:*
"heus, Poenica![4]"

Poenica, caeca, vidēre nōn potest.
sed, vidētur Poenicae esse[5] Rūfum.

---

[3] **Rūfō in tabernā** *with Rufus in the shop*
[4] **heus, Poenica!** *Hey, Poenica!*
[5] **vidētur Poenicae esse** *it seems to Poenica that it's*

*Poenica:*
"Rūfe?"

*Rūfus:*
"sum!"[6]


in tabernā Poenicae,
Rūfus videt multās togās.
togae excellenter purpurātae sunt.
Rūfō colōrēs placent.
colōrēs purpureī Rūfō valdē placent.


*Rūfus:*
"Poenica, volō
togam purpuream."

---

[6] **sum!** *It's me!*

# III
# togae et mūricēs

Rūfus in tabernā Poenicae est.
Rūfus togam purpuream vult.

*Poenica:*
"Rūfe, habeō multās
togās purpureās in tabernā."

*Rūfus:*
"excellēns!
gerō togam praetextam.[1]
habēsne togās praetextās?"

---

[1] **gerō togam praetextam** *I wear the toga praetexta
(i.e. toga with a purple-striped border that young boys
from more-privileged families wore).*

*Poenica:*
"hmm, habeō multās togās purpureās.
sed, nōn habeō togās praetextās.
sed, purpurāre togam praetextam
difficile nōn est."

*Rūfus:*
"excellēns!"

*Poenica:*
"Rūfe, nōn est difficile
purpurāre togam praetextam.
sed, nōn habeō multōs mūricēs.[2]"

*Rūfus:*
"nōn habēs mūricēs?"

---

[2] **mūricēs** *the sea snails that purple dye came from*

*Poenica:*
"habeō mūricēs,
sed nōn habeō *multōs* mūricēs.
purpurāre togam praetextam
est $\overline{\text{XII}}$ mūricum.[3]
volō $\overline{\text{XII}}$ mūricum."

*Rūfus:*
"$\overline{\text{XII}}$ mūricum sunt multī!
nōn habeō mūricēs.
sed, ferunt 'Sextum habēre[4] mūricēs.'"

---

[3] $\overline{\text{XII}}$ **mūricum** *12,000 sea snails*
[4] **ferunt 'Sextum habēre...'** *they say that Sextus has...*

*Poenica:*
"Sextus mūricēs habet?!"

*Rūfus:*
"ferunt..."

*Poenica:*
"excellēns!"

subitō, Rūfus videt fūnem!

*Rūfus:*
"Poenica, estne...*fūnis*
...in tabernā?!"

*Poenica:*
"est! volō fūnambula esse."

*Rūfus:*
"vīsne esse fūnambula?!
sed, Poenica, es purpurāria excellēns!"

*Poenica:*
"purpurāria sum.
sed, quoque volō esse fūnambula."

*Rūfus:*
"volō attemptāre
ambulāre in fūnem quoque."

*Poenica:*
"Rūfe, cautē ambulā in fūnem!
difficile—nōn—diffiCILLIMUM est
ambulāre in fūnem."

Rūfus ambulāre in fūnem attemptat.
sed, Rūfus cautus nōn est.

subitō, Rūfus cadit!

# IV
# Sextus

Poenica est purpurāria excellēns.
sed, Poenica fūnambula vult esse.
in tabernā, Poenica vult
ambulāre in fūnem.

caeca, Poenica cauta est.
Poenica in fūnem ambulāre attemptat.

subitō, Sextus in tabernam
Poenicae ambulat!

Sextō in tabernā,[1]
Poenica nōn ambulat in fūnem.

---

[1] **Sextō in tabernā** *with Sextus in the shop*

Poenica impatiēns est.

in tabernā Poenicae,
Sextus videt multās togās.
togae vīvidae
excellenter purpurātae sunt.


colōrēs Sextō placent.
colōrēs purpureī Sextō valdē placent.
sed, Sextus togam purpuream
nōn gerit.
Sextus fert mūricēs
ad togam Rūfī purpurandam.[2]
Sextus Poenicam videt.


*Sextus:*
"heus, Poenica!"


Poenica, caeca,
Sextum vidēre nōn potest.

---

[2] **ad togam purpurandam** *for the toga to be purpled*

sed, vidētur Poenicae esse[3] Sextum.

Poenica:
"Sexte?"

Sextus:
"sum! habeō togam et mūricēs."

Poenica:
"excellēns!
Rūfus voluit togam praetextam.
volō purpurāre
togam praetextam Rūfō.
suntne mūricēs Tyriī?"[4]

Sextus:
"habeō mūricēs Tyriōs multōs!
ferō mūricēs
ad togam Rūfī purpurandam."

---

[3] **vidētur Poenicae esse** *it seems to Poenica that it's*
[4] **Tyriī** *Tyrian, from Tyre (i.e. Labanon), where sea snails for dyeing came from*

*Poenica:*
"excellēns!
toga Rūfī purpurābitur
in septimānā.[5]"

Poenica purpurātūra est[6] togam.

subitō, Sextus videt fūnem!

---

[5] **in septimānā** *within a week*
[6] **purpurātūra est** *is about to purple*

# V
# Poenica, rīdiculum est!

in tabernā Poenicae,
Sextus fūnem vīdit.

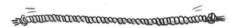

*Sextus:*
"Poenica, habēs
fūnem in tabernā?!"

*Poenica:*
"habeō!
volō esse fūnambula."

*Sextus:*
"Poenica, rīdiculum est!
es purpurāria excellēns.
sed, vīs esse fūnambula?!"

*Poenica:*
"rīdiculum nōn est!
volō esse fūnambula
*et quoque* purpurāria."

fūnambulī Sextō placent—nōn—
VALDĒ placent!

*Sextus:*
"fūnambulī sunt extraōrdināriī!
Poenica, ambulā in fūnem!"

subitō, Poenica cautē
in fūnem ambulat!
Poenica in fūnem
excellenter ambulat!
Poenica nōn cadit.

*Sextus:*
"extraōrdinārium!
volō attemptāre
in fūnem ambulāre quoque."

*Poenica:*
"ambulāvistīne[1] in fūnem?
esne āthlēticus?"

*Sextus:*
"in fūnem nōn ambulāvī.
nōn sum āthlēticus."

*Poenica:*
"Sexte, ambulāre in fūnem
difficillimum est!
āthlētica sum.
possum ambulāre in fūnem."

---

[1] **ambulāvistīne...?** *Have you ever walked...?*

*Sextus:*
"difficillimum est? cautus erō.[2]
volō attemptāre in fūnem ambulāre."


Sextus in fūnem ambulāre attemptat.
sed, Sextus in fūnem
ambulāre nōn potest!
Sextus cautus, sed nōn āthlēticus est.


subitō, Sextus cadit!

---

# VI
# Terrex Extraōrdinārius

Poenica in fūnem
ambulāre attemptāvit.
sed, multī Rōmānī in tabernā erant.
Rōmānīs in tabernā,[1]
Poenica in fūnem ambulāre nōn potuit.
Poenica impatiēns est.

*Poenica:*
"Rōmānīs multīs in tabernā,
fūnambula nōn erō!"[2]

Poenica in fūnem ambulātūra est.[3]

---

[1] **Rōmānīs in tabernā** *with Romans in the shop*
[2] **fūnambula nōn erō** *I'll never be a tightrope walker*
[3] **ambulātūra est** *is about to walk*

subitō, Rōmānus
in tabernam Poenicae
ambulat!

Poenica impatientissima est.
Rōmānus Poenicam videt.

*Rōmānus:*
"heus, purpurāria!"

Poenica, caeca,
Rōmānum vidēre nōn potest.

*Poenica:*
"Tiberī?"

*Rōmānus:*
"Tiberius nōn sum. Terrex sum.
sum Terrex Extraōrdinārius!
nōn vidēs Terregem Extraōrdinārium?!"

*Poenica:*
"caeca sum.
nōn possum vidēre."


*Terrex:*
"purpurāria caeca?!
extraōrdinārium!"


ferunt 'Terregem esse[4]
Rōmānum rīdiculum.'
vidētur Poenicae Terregem esse
Rōmānum rīdicuLISSIMUM!
Poenicae Terrex nōn placet.
sed, Terrex in tabernā Poenicae est.


in tabernā Poenicae,
Terrex togās multās purpureās
vīvidās et excellentēs videt.
colōrēs vīvidī Terregī placent.
colōrēs purpureī Terregī valdē placent.

---

[4] **ferunt 'Terregem esse...'** *They say Terrex is...*

Terregī pretiōsa—nōn—
pretiōSISSIMA[5] placent.
togae purpureae pretiōsissimae sunt.
Terrex togam purpurārī valdē vult.


*Terrex:*
"habeō togam.
volō togam purpurārī.
potesne purpurāre togam?
volō habēre togam pictam.[6]"

---

5 **pretiōSISSIMA** *really precious things*
6 **togam pictam** *super fancy embroidered toga*
*reserved for consuls, emperors, triumphs, etc.*

29

*Poenica:*
"purpurāria sum.
possum purpurāre togās multās.
sed, vīs togam...*pictam?!*
esne...cōnsul?"

Terrex cōnsul nōn est.
Terrex impatiēns est...

# VII
## Terrex Tyrius

*Terrex, impatienter:*
"cōnsul...nōn sum.
sed, volō habēre
togam pictam."

Terrex togam pictam valdē vult.
sed, cōnsulēs togās pictās gerunt.
Terrex cōnsul nōn est.
Terrex nōn potest gerere
togam pictam.
Poenica attemptat persuādēre Terregī.

*Poenica:*
"cōnsulēs togās pictās gerunt.
sed, cōnsul nōn es.
nōn potes gerere togam pictam."

Terrex nōn persuādētur.


*Terrex, impatientissimē:*
"nōn sum cōnsul.
sed, Terrex Extraōrdinārius sum.
gerō multās togās.
gerō togās praetextās.
gerō togās extraōrdināriās.
gerō togās multīs colōribus,
et gerō togās purpureās!
gerō pretiōsa.
gerō pretiōsissima!
gerō togās purpureās vīvidās et
extraōrdināriās et pretiōsissimās!
sum Terrex Tyrius!
volō habēre togam pictam Tyriam!" [1]

Terrex togam pictam Tyriam
gerere nōn potest.

---

[1] **Tyriam** *"Tyrian" can also mean "purple" on its own.*

Poenica attemptāvit
persuādēre Terregī.
sed, Poenica purpurāria est,
et Terrex togam pictam valdē vult.
Poenica purpurābit togam Terregī.


*Poenica:*
"possum togam pictam purpurāre."


*Terrex:*
"excellēns!"


*Poenica:*
"toga picta purpurābitur
in septimānīs multīs.[2]"

*Terrex, impatientissimē:*
"in septimānīs...*multīs?!*"

---

[2] **in septimānīs multīs** *within many weeks*

*Poenica, impatienter:*
"purpurāre togam pictam
difficile—nōn—diffiCILLIMUM est!
purpurāria sum.
sed...nōn habeō mūricēs
ad togam pictam purpurandam."

*Terrex:*
"nōn habēs mūricēs?!
habeō mūricēs.
habeō mūricēs multōs.
sum Terrex!
sum Terrex Tyrius Extraōrdinārius!
volō togās Tyriās!
volōōōō togāāāās Tyriāāāās!"

*Poenica:*
"habēs...'multōs' mūricēs?
purpurāre togam praetextam
est $\overline{XII}$ mūricum...

...purpurāre togam pictam
est...$\overline{\text{CCL}}$...mūricum!³
habēsne $\overline{\text{CCL}}$ mūricum?!"

*Terrex:*
"sum Terrex Extraōrdinārius!
feram mūricum $\overline{\text{CCL}}$
ad togam pictam purpurandam!"

---

³ $\overline{\text{CCL}}$**...mūricum!** *250,000 sea snails!*

subitō, Terrex fūnem in tabernā videt!

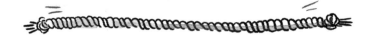

*Terrex:*
"estne...estne...*fūnis*?!"

# VIII
## āthlēticus nōn est

in tabernā Poenicae,
Terrex fūnem vīdit.

*Poenica, impatiēns:*
"est fūnis.
habeō fūnem in tabernā.
sum purpurāria.
sed, quoque volō esse fūnambula."

fūnambulī Terregī valdē placent.

*Terrex:*
"purpurāria *et* fūnambula
caeca?! extraōrdinārium!"

Poenicae nōn placet Terrex.

*Terrex:*
"fūnambulī sunt extraōrdināriī!
quoque volō in fūnem ambulāre!"

*Poenica:*
"ambulāvistīne in fūnem?
difficillimum e—"

sed, Terrex subitō in fūnem ambulat!

Terrex cautus nōn est.
Terrex āthlēticus nōn est.
Terrex in fūnem ambulāre nōn potest.
est rīdiculum!

subitō, Terrex cadit!

*Poenica...
excellēns!*

# IX
# Vestālis

Poenica in fūnem
ambulāre attemptāvit.
sed, Terrex et multī Rōmānī
in tabernam ambulāvērunt.
Rōmānīs in tabernā, Poenica
in fūnem ambulāre nōn potuit.
Poenica in fūnem ambulātūra est.

subitō, Vestālis[1]
in tabernam Poenicae
ambulat!

Vestālis Poenicam videt.

---

[1] **Vestālis** *Vestal, a sacred, highly honored Roman priestess*

*Vestālis:*
"heus, purpurāria!"

caeca, Poenica Vestālem
vidēre nōn potest.
sed, vidētur Poenicae esse Vestālem.

*Poenica:*
"heus, Vestālis!"

in tabernā Poenicae,
Vestālis videt togās Tyriās.
Poenica multās togās Tyriās habet.

*Vestālis:*
"Poenica, purpurāria excellēns es.
purpurāvistī togās multās!
in tabernā, habēs
vīvidās togās Tyriās.
sed, nōn videō suffībula.[2]"

---

[2] **suffībula** *special veils with purple trim that Vestals wore*

Vestālēs suffībula gerunt.
in suffībulō color purpureus est.
Vestālis vult Poenicam
suffībulum purpurāre.


*Vestālis:*
"Poenica, habeō suffībulum
ad purpurandum.
potesne purpurāre suffībulum?"


*Poenica:*
"purpurāre suffībulum
difficile nōn est."


*Vestālis:*
"excellēns! nōn difficile est?"

*Poenica:*
"nōn est.
purpurāre togam *pictam*
est difficillimum, et $\overline{CCL}$ mūricum...

...purpurāre togam *praetextam* est difficile, et $\overline{XII}$ mūricum. sed, purpurāre suffībulum nōn difficile, et $\overline{III}$ mūricum[3] est. $\overline{III}$ mūricum multī nōn sunt. habeō mūricum $\overline{III}$ ...

$\overline{III}$ mūricum

$\overline{XII}$ mūricum

$\overline{CCL}$ mūricum

...suffībulum in septimānā purpurābitur."

*Vestālis:*
"excellēns!"

---

[3] $\overline{III}$ **mūricum** *3,000 sea snails*

# X
# esse fūnambulum

esse fūnambulum
difficile erat Poenicae.
sed, septimānās multās,[1]
Rōmānī in tabernam Poenicae
nōn ambulāvērunt.
sed quoque, nōn est extraōrdinārium.
colōrēs Tyriī sunt pretiōsī.
multī Rōmānī nōn gerunt Tyria.
multī Rōmānī nōn possunt
habēre Tyria.
Rōmānīs nōn in tabernā,
Poenica ambulāre in fūnem potest.
Poenica in fūnem ambulātūra est.

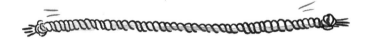

---

[1] **septimānās multās** *after many weeks*

subitō, in tabernam
Poenicae ambulat...
gladiātor!

gladiātor Poenicam videt.

*gladiātor:*
"heus, Poenica purpurāria!"

Poenica, caeca,
gladiātōrem vidēre nōn potest.
vidētur Poenicae esse
gladiātōrem Carpophorum.

*Poenica:*
"Carpophore?"

*gladiātor:*
"nōn sum Carpophorus.
sum Crixaflamma!"

ferunt 'Crixaflammam esse[2]
gladiātōrem excellentem.'

> Poenica:
> "Crixaflamma?!
> gladiātor excellēns es!"

Crixaflamma:
"gladiātor excellēns *eram*."

> Poenica...
> *Crixaflamma gladiātor **erat**,*
> *sed nōn **est** gladiātor.*
> *vultne Crixaflamma...togam?!*

> Poenica:
> "sum purpurāria.
> vīsne togam purpuream?"

---

[2] **ferunt 'Crixaflammam esse...'** *They say that*
*Crixaflamma is...*

*Crixaflamma:*
"nōn gerō togās.
sed...volō esse fūnambulus!
ferunt 'Poenicam purpurāriam
quoque esse fūnambulam.'
volō in fūnem ambulāre quoque!"

*Poenica:*
"extraōrdinārium!
sed, potesne ambulāre in fūnem?
esne āthlēticus?"

*Crixaflamma:*
"sum gladiātor!
gladiātōrēs āthlēticī—nōn—
āthlētiCISSIMĪ sunt!
possum in fūnem ambulāre."

Crixaflamma cautē
et āthlēticē
in fūnem ambulat.
Crixaflamma in fūnem
excellenter ambulat!

Crixaflamma nōn cadit.

Crixaflammae,
difficile nōn est ambulāre in fūnem.
extraōrdinārium!
Poenica quoque
in fūnem ambulātūra est.

subitō, Oenobatiātus[3]
in tabernam ambulat!

---

[3] **Oenobatiātus** *Crixaflamma's gladiator trainer*

# XI
# fūnambulī

*Oenobatiātus:*
"heus, Crixaflamma!"

*Crixaflamma:*
"Oenobatiāte!"

*Oenobatiātus:*
"Crixaflamma,
es in tabernā purpurāriae.
sed, gladiātōrēs togās nōn gerunt!
quoque, ferunt 'Crixaflammam
nōn velle[1] esse gladiātōrem!'
rīdiculum est!"

---

[1] **ferunt 'Crixaflammam nōn velle...'** *They say that Crixaflamma doesn't want*

subitō, Oenobatiātus fūnem videt!

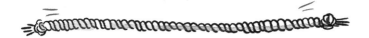

Crixaflamma videt
Oenobatiātum esse impatientem.


*Crixaflamma:*
"Oenobatiāte, gladiātor eram.
sed, volō esse fūnambulus."


*Oenobatiātus, impatienter:*
"fūnambulus?!
sed, gladiātor excellēns es!
gladiātōrēs excellentēs
pretiōSISSIMĪ sunt!"


Poenica vult Crixaflammam
esse fūnambulum quoque.
Poenica vult persuādēre Oenobatiātō.

*Poenica, cautē*
*Oenobatiātō persuādēns:*
"Oenobatiāte, sum purpurāria,
et quoque possum in fūnem ambulāre.
volō esse purpurāria...*et*...fūnambula.
potestne Crixaflamma esse
gladiātor...*et*...fūnambulus?
fūnambulī quoque
possunt esse pretiōsissimī."

*Oenobatiātus:*
"fūnambulī possunt
esse...pretiōsissimī?"

*Poenica:*
"ferunt..."

Crixaflamma videt Oenobatiātum
nōn esse impatientem.
Crixaflamma valdē vult
esse fūnambulus.

Crixaflamma vult Poenicam
esse fūnambulam quoque.
Crixaflamma attemptat
persuādēre Oenobatiātō.


*Crixaflamma, Oenobatiātō persuādēns:*
"...et Poenica extraōrdināria
purpurāria et fūnambula est.
Poenica caeca est.
Poenica nōn potest vidēre.
sed, Poenica potest purpurāre togās
et suffībula, et Poenica quoque
potest in fūnem ambulāre, caeca!"


Oenobatiātus videt
Poenicam, et Crixaflammam.


*Oenobatiātus:*
"purpurāria caeca fūnambula,
et fūnambulus gladiātor.
extraōrdinārium!
Crixaflamma, potes esse
gladiātor...*et*...fūnambulus."

# Oenobatiātus persuādētur!

*Crixaflamma:*
"Poenica, sīmus fūnambulī!"[2]

*Poenica:*
"fūnambulī sīmus!"

*Oenobatiātus:*
"excellēns!"

---

[2] **sīmus fūnambulī!** *Let's be tightrope walkers!*

# Index Verbōrum

## 1,2,3

| | |
|---|---|
| II | *2* |
| II̅/MM | *2,000* |
| III | *3* |
| III̅/MMM | *3,000* |
| X | *10* |
| X̅ | *10,000* |
| XII̅ | *12,000* |
| L | *50* |
| L̅ | *50,000* |
| CC | *200* |
| CC̅ | *200,000* |
| CCL̅ | *250,000* |

## A

**ad** *towards, to*
**ambulā!** *Walk!*
    cautē ambulā! *Walk cautiously!*
  **ambulāre** *to walk*
    ambulāre in fūnem *to walk on a rope*
  **ambulat** *walks*
    in tabernam ambulat *walks into the shop*
    nōn ambulat in fūnem *doesn't walk on the rope*
  **ambulātūra est** *about to walk*
    Poenica ambulātūra est *Poenica is about to walk*
  **ambulāvērunt** *they walked*
    in tabernam ambulāvērunt *walked into the shop*
  **ambulāvī** *I walked*
    nōn ambulāvī *I haven't walked*
  **ambulāvistīne?** *Have you walked?*
    ambulāvistīne in fūnem? *Have you ever walked on a rope?*
**āthlētica** *athletic*
    āthlētica sum *I'm athletic*
  **āthlēticē** *athletically*

**āthlēticī** *athletic*
    gladiātōrēs āthlēticī *athletic gladiators*
**āthlēticissimī** *very athletic*
    gladiātōrēs āthlēticīssimī sunt *gladiators are very athletic*
**āthlēticus** *athletic*
    nōn sum āthlēticus *I'm not athletic*
**attemptāre** *to attempt (i.e. to try)*
    attemptāre in fūnem ambulāre *to attempt to walk on a rope*
  **attemptat** *attempts*
    ambulāre in fūnem attemptat *attempts to walk on a rope*
    attemptat persuādēre *attempts to persuade*
  **attemptāvit** *tried*
    ambulāre in fūnem attemptāvit *tried to walk on a rope*
    attemptāvit persuādēre *tried to persuade*

# C

**cadit** *falls*
    nōn cadit *doesn't fall*
**caeca** *blind*
    caeca sum *I'm blind*
    purpurāria caeca *a blind purple-dyer*
**Carpophore** *Carphorus, Crixaflamma's gladiatorial rival*
    Carpophore "Carpophorus..." *(i.e. speaking to Carpophorus)*
  **Carpophorum** *Carphorus*
    vidētur esse Carpophorum *it seems to be Carphorus*
  **Carpophorus**
**cauta** *cautious (i.e. careful)*
  **cautē** *cautiously*
  **cautus** *cautious*
    cautus erō *I'll be cautious*
**color** *color*
  **colōrēs** *colors*
    placent colōrēs *like colors*
    colōrēs Tyriī *Tyrian colors*
  **colōribus** *colors*
    multīs colōribus *of many colors*
**cōnsul** *consul, the highest level of Roman government*
    esne...cōnsul?! *What are you...a consul?!*
    cōnsul nōn est *isn't a consul*
  **cōnsulēs** *consuls*
**Crixaflamma** *Crixaflamma, the best gladiator around*
  **Crixaflammae** *for Crixaflamma*

Crixaflammae, difficile nōn est *for Crixaflamma, it's not difficult*
**Crixaflammam** *Crixaflamma*
>ferunt 'Crixaflammam esse...' *They say Crixaflamma is...*
>ferunt 'Crixaflammam nōn velle...' *They say that Crixaflamma doesn't want*
>vult Crixaflammam esse *wants Crixaflamma to be*
>videt Crixaflammam *sees Crixaflamma*

# D, E

**difficile** *difficult*
>**difficillimum** *really difficult, most difficult*

**eram** *I was*
>**erant** *they were*
>**erat** *was*
>**erō** *I will be*
>**es** *you are*
>**esne?** *Are you?*
>**esse** *to be*
>>vidētur Poenicae esse *it seems to Poenica that it's*
>>ferunt 'Terregem esse...' *They say Terrex is...*
>>ferunt 'Crixaflammam esse...' *They say Crixaflamma is...*
>>videt Oenobatiātum esse *sees that Oenobatiatus is*
>**est** *is*
>**estne?** *Is?*

**excellēns** *excellent*
>>purpurāria excellēns *excellent purple-dyer*
>>excellēns! *How excellent!*
>>gladiātor excellēns *excellent gladiator*
>**excellentem** *excellent*
>>esse gladiātōrem excellentem *to be an excellent gladiator*
>**excellenter** *excellently*
>**excellentēs** *excellent*
>>videt togās excellentēs *sees excellent togas*
>>gladiātōrēs excellentēs *excellent gladiators*

**extraōrdināria** *extraordinary*
>>purpurāria extraōrdināria *an extraordinary purple-dyer*
>>fūnambula extraōrdināria *extraordinary tightrope walker*
>**extraōrdināriās** *extraordinary*
>>gerō togās extraōrdināriās *I wear extraordinary togas*
>**extraōrdināriī** *extraordinary*
>>colōrēs extraōrdināriī *extraordinary colors*
>>fūnambulī extraōrdināriī *extraordinary tightrope walkers*

**extraōrdinārium** *extraordinary*

    extraōrdinārium! *How extraordinary!*

    nōn vidēs Terregem Extraōrdinārium?! *You don't see*
                                   *Extraordinary Terrex?!*

**extraōrdinārius** *extraordinary*

    sum Terrex Extraōrdinārius! *I'm Extraordinary Terrex!*

# F

**feram** *I will bring*

    feram mūricēs *I'll bring sea snails*

**ferō** *I bring*

    ferō mūricēs *I bring sea snails*

**fert** *brings*

    fert mūricēs *brings sea snails*

**ferunt** *they say (i.e. they carry the message that...)*

    ferunt 'Sextum habēre...' *They say that Sextus has...*

    ferunt 'Terregem esse...' *They say Terrex is...*

    ferunt 'Crixaflammam esse...' *They say Crixaflamma is...*

    ferunt 'Poenicam esse...' *They say Poenica is...*

    ferunt 'Crixaflammam nōn velle...' *They say that*
                                 *Crixaflamma doesn't want*

    ferunt... *so they say...*

**fūnambula** *tightrope walker*

    vult esse fūnambula *wants to be a tightrope walker*

    fūnambula nōn erō *I'll never be a tightrope walker*

    fūnambula caeca *a blind tightrope walker*

**fūnambulam** *tightrope walker*

    esse fūnambulam *to be a tightrope walker*

**fūnambulī** *tightrope walkers*

    fūnambulī placent *likes tightrope walkers*

    sīmus fūnambulī! *Let's be tightrope walkers!*

**fūnambulum** *tightrope walker*

    esse fūnambulum *to be a tightrope walker*

**fūnambulus** *tightrope walker*

    vult esse fūnambulus *wants to be a tightrope walker*

**fūnem** *rope*

    fūnem habēre *to have a rope*

    ambulāre in fūnem *to walk on a rope*

    vidēre fūnem *to see a rope*

**fūnis** *rope*

# G, H

**gerere** *to wear*

    gerere togam pictam *to wear the toga picta*

  **gerit** *wears*

    togam purpuream nōn gerit *doesn't wear a purple toga*

  **gerō** *I wear*

    gerō togam praetextam *I wear the toga praetexta*

    gerō togās *I wear togas*

    gerō pretiōsa *I wear precious things*

  **gerunt** *they wear*

    togās nōn gerunt *don't wear togas*

    togās pictās gerunt *wear embroidered togas*

    suffībula gerunt *wear veils*

    nōn gerunt Tyria *don't wear Tyrian (i.e. purple) things*

**gladiātor** *gladiator (i.e. arena fighter)*

  **gladiātōrem** *gladiator*

    gladiātōrem vidēre *to see a gladiator*

    vidētur esse gladiātōrem *seems to be a gladiator*

    esse gladiātōrem excellentem *to be an excellent gladiator*

  **gladiātōrēs** *gladiators*

**habeō** *I have*

    habeō togās *I have togas*

    nōn habeō mūricēs *I don't have sea snails*

    "habeō!" "*I do have it!*"

    habeō suffībulum *I have a veil*

  **habēre** *to have*

    ferunt 'Sextum habēre...' *They say that Sextus has...*

    habēre togam *to have a toga*

    nōn possunt habēre *aren't able to have*

  **habēs** *you have*

    nōn habēs mūricēs? *You don't have sea snails?*

    habēs fūnem?! *You have a rope?!*

    habēs 'multōs' mūricēs?! *You have "many" sea snails?!*

    habēs vīvidās togās Tyriās *you have vivid Tyrian togas*

  **habēsne?** *Do you have?*

    habēsne togās praetextās? *Do you have toga praetextas?*

  **habet** *has*

    tabernam habet *has a shop*

    fūnem habet *has a rope*

    mūricēs habet *has sea snails*

    multās togās Tyriās habet *has many Tyrian togas*

**heus!** *Hey!*

# I, M, N, O, P

**impatiēns** *impatient*
  **impatientem** *impatient*
    esse impatientem *being impatient*
  **impatienter** *impatiently*
  **impatientissima** *really impatient*
  **impatientissimē** *really impatiently*
**in** *in, on, into*
**multās** *many*
      multās togās purpurat *purples many togas*
      videt multās togās *sees many togas*
      habēre multās togās *to have many togas*
      gerō multās togās *I wear many togas*
      septimānās multās *after many weeks*
  **multī** *many*
    multī colōrēs *many colors*
    multī Rōmānī *many Romans*
    multī mūricēs *many sea snails*
  **multīs** *many*
    multīs colōribus *of many colors*
    in septimānīs multīs *within many weeks*
  **multōs** *many*
    habēre multōs mūricēs *to have many sea snails*
**mūricēs** *the sea snails that purple dye came from*
    habēre mūricēs *to have sea snails*
    ferre mūricēs *to bring sea snails*
**nōn** *not, doesn't*
**Oenobatiāte** *Oenobatiatus, Crixaflamma's gladiator trainer*
    Oenobatiāte *"Oenobatiatus..." (i.e. speaking to Oenobatiatus)*
  **Oenobatiātō** *Oenobatiatus*
    persuādēre Oenobatiātō *to persuade Oenobatiatus*
  **Oenobatiātum** *Oenobatiatus*
    videt Oenobatiātum esse *sees that Oenobatiatus is*
  **Oenobatiātus** *Oenobatiatus*
**persuādēns** *persuading*
    persuādēns Oenobatiātō *persuading Oenobatiatus*
  **persuādēre** *to persuade*
    persuādēre Terregī *to persuade Terrex*
    persuādēre Oenobatiātō *to persuade Oenobatiatus*
  **persuādētur** *is persuaded*
    persuādētur nōn est *isn't persuaded*
**picta** *toga picta (i.e. super fancy embroidered toga reserved*
                    *for consuls, emperors, triumphs, etc.*

**pictam** *embroidered toga*
    habēre togam pictam *to have an embroidered toga*
**pictās** *embroidered*
    togās pictās gerunt *wear embroidered togas*
**placent** *likes [more than one thing]*
    Poenicae placent *Poenica likes*
    Rōmānīs placent *Romans like*
    Rūfō placent *Rūfus likes*
    Sextō placent *Sextus likes*
    valdē placent *really likes*
    Terregī placent *Terrex likes*
**placet** *likes*
    Terrex nōn placet *doesn't like Terrex*
**Poenica** *our immigrant purple-dyer from Tyre (i.e. Lebanon),*
    *also means "Phoenician," the people of ancient Lebanon,*
    *and stands for "purple" on its own*
**Poenicae** *Poenica's, Poenica*
    in tabernā Poenicae *in Poenica's shop*
    in tabernam Poenicae *into Poenica's shop*
    vidētur Poenicae *it seems to Poenica that*
    Poenicae nōn placet *Poenica doesn't like*
**Poenicam** *Poenica*
    Poenicam videt *sees Poenica*
    vult Poenicam purpurāre *wants Poenica to purple*
    ferunt 'Poenicam esse...' *They say Poenica is...*
    vult Poenicam esse *wants Poenica to be*
**possum** *I'm able, I can*
    possum ambulāre in fūnem *I can walk on a rope*
    nōn possum vidēre *I'm not able to see*
    possum purpurāre togās *I'm able to purple togas*
**possunt** *they are able, they can*
    nōn possunt habēre *can't have*
    possunt esse pretiōsissimī *can be really valuable*
**potes** *you are able, you can*
    nōn potes gerere *you can't wear*
    potes esse *you're able to be*
**potesne?** *Are you able?, Can you?*
    potesne purpurāre? *Can you purple?*
**potest** *is able, can*
    nōn potest vidēre *isn't able to see*
    ambulāre in fūnem nōn potest *isn't able to walk on a rope*
    nōn potest gerere *isn't able to wear*
**potestne?** *Is able?*

potestne esse? *Is he able to be?*
**potuit** *was able*
    in fūnem ambulāre nōn potuit *wasn't able to walk on a rope*
**praetextam** *toga praetexta, a toga with a purple-striped border*
        *that young boys from more-privileged families wore*
    gerō togam praetextam *I wear the toga praetexta*
    purpurāre togam praetextam *to purple a toga praetexta*
    voluit togam praetextam *wanted toga praetexta*
**praetextās** *toga praetextas*
    habēre togās praetextās *to have toga praetextas*
    gerō togās praetextās *I wear toga praetextas*
**pretiōsa** *precious things (i.e. valuable, expensive)*
    gerō pretiōsa *I wear precious things*
**pretiōsī** *precious*
    colōrēs purpureī pretiōsī *precious purple colors*
    colōrēs Tyriī pretiōsī *precious Tyrian colors*
**pretiōsissima** *really precious, expensive things*
    pretiōsissima placent *likes really precious things*
    gerō pretiōsissima *I wear really expensive things*
**pretiōsissimae** *really precious*
    togae purpureae pretiōsissimae *really precious purple togas*
**pretiōsissimās** *really expensive*
    gerō togās pretiōsissimās *I wear really expensive togas*
**pretiōsissimī** *really valuable*
    gladiātōrēs pretiōsissimī *really valuable gladiators*
    possunt esse pretiōsissimī *they can be really valuable*
**purpurābit** *will purple (i.e. will dye purple)*
    purpurābit togam Terregī *will purple a toga for Terrex*
**purpurābitur** *will be purpled*
    purpurābitur in septimānā *will be purpled within a week*
**purpurandam** *being purpled*
    ad togam purpurandam *for purpling a toga*
**purpurandum** *being purpled*
    suffībulum ad purpurandum *a veil to be purpled*
**purpurāre** *to purple*
    purpurāre togam *to purple a toga*
    suffībulum purpurāre *to purple a veil*
**purpurārī** *to be purpled*
    togam purpurārī vult *wants a toga to be purpled*
**purpurat** *purples*
    togās purpurat *purples togas*
**purpurātae sunt** *were purpled*
    togae purpurātae sunt *togas were purpled*

**purpurātūra est** *about to purple*
    purpurātūra est togam *is about to purple the toga*
**purpurāvistī** *you have purpled*
    purpurāvistī togās multās *you've purpled many togas*
**purpurāria** *a purple-dyer (i.e. someone who dyes clothes purple)*
    vult esse purpurāria *wants to be a purple-dyer*
**purpurāriae** *of a purple-dyer*
    in tabernā purpurāriae *in the shop of a purple-dyer*
**purpurāriam** *purple-dyer*
    ferunt 'purpurāriam esse...' *They say the purple-dyer is...*
**purpureae** *purple*
    togae purpureae *purple togas*
**purpuream** *purple*
    velle togam purpuream *to want a purple toga*
    togam purpuream nōn gerit *doesn't wear a purple toga*
**purpureās** *purple*
    volunt togās purpureās *they want purple togas*
    habeō multās togās purpureās *I have many purple togas*
    videt togās purpureās *sees purple togas*
    gerō togās purpureās *I wear purple togas*
**purpureī** *purple*
    colōrēs purpureī *purple colors*
**purpureus** *purple*
    color purpureus *purple color*

# Q, R
**quoque** *also*
**rīdiculissimum** *really ridiculous, most ridiculous*
    esse rīdiculissimum *being the most ridiculous*
**rīdiculum** *ridiculous*
    est rīdiculum! *It's ridiculous!*
    esse Rōmānum rīdiculum *being a ridiculous Roman*
**Rōmae** *in Rome*
**Rōmānī** *Romans*
  **Rōmānīs** *Romans*
    Rōmānīs placent *Romans like*
    Rōmānīs in tabernā *with Romans in the shop*
  **Rōmānum** *the Roman*
    Rōmānum vidēre *to see the Roman*
    esse Rōmānum rīdiculum *being a ridiculous Roman*
  **Rōmānus** *a Roman*
**Rūfe** *"Rufus..." (i.e. speaking to Rufus)*

**Rūfī** *of Rufus*
> ad togam Rūfī purpurandam *for purpling Rufus' toga*
> toga Rūfī *Rufus' toga*

**Rūfō** *Rufus*
> Rūfō in tabernā *with Rufus in the shop*
> Rūfō placent *Rufus likes*
> purpurāre togam Rūfō *to purple a toga for Rufus*

**Rūfum** *Rufus*
> vidētur esse Rūfum *it seems that it's Rufus*

**Rūfus** *Rufus, Sextus' friend*


# S

**sed** *but*

**septimānā** *a week*
> purpurābitur in septimānā *will be purpled within a week*

**septimānās** *weeks*
> septimānās multās *after many weeks*

**septimānīs** *weeks*
> in septimānīs multīs *within many weeks*

**Sexte** *"Sextus..." (i.e. speaking to Sextus)*

**Sextō** *Sextus*
> Sextō in tabernā *with Sextus in the shop*
> Sextō placent *Sextus likes*

**Sextum** *Sextus, friend of Rufus*
> ferunt 'Sextum habēre...' *They say that Sextus has...*
> Sextum vidēre *to see Sextus*
> vidētur esse Sextum *it seems that it's Sextus*

**Sextus** *Sextus*

**sīmus!** *Let's be!*
> sīmus fūnambulī! *Let's be tightrope walkers!*

**subitō!** *Suddenly!*

**suffībula** *special veils with purple trim that Vestals wore*
> nōn videō suffībula *I don't see any veils*
> suffībula gerunt *wear veils*
> purpurāre suffībula *to purple veils*

**suffībulō** *veil*
> in suffībulō *on the veil*

**suffībulum** *veil*
> suffībulum purpurāre *to purple a veil*
> habeō suffībulum *I have a veil*

**sum** *I am*
> "sum!" *"It's me!"*

**sunt** *there are, they are*
**suntne?** *Are?*


# T

**tabernā** *a shop*
> in tabernā Poenicae *in Poenica's shop*
> Rūfō in tabernā *with Rufus in the shop*
> Sextō in tabernā *with Sextus in the shop*
> Rōmānīs in tabernā *with Romans in the shop*

**tabernam** *a shop*
> tabernam habet *has a shop*
> in tabernam ambulat *walks into the shop*

**Terregem** *Terrex, an arrogant Roman who's basically a big jerk*
> nōn vidēs Terregem Extraōrdinārium?! *You don't see*
> The Extraordinary Terrex?!
> ferunt 'Terregem esse...' *They say Terrex is...*
> vidētur Terregem esse *it seems that Terrex is*

**Terregī** *Terrex*
> Terregī placent *Terrex likes*
> persuādēre Terregī *to persuade Terrex*
> purpurābit togam Terregī *will purple a toga for Terrex*

**Terrex** *Terrex*

**Tiberī** *"Tiberius..." (i.e. speaking to Tiberius, Rufus' father)*

**Tiberius** *Tiberius*

**toga** *toga, the Roman cothing*

**togae** *togas*

**togam** *toga*
> velle togam *to want a toga*
> gerere togam purpuream *to wear a purple toga*
> purpurāre togam *to purple a toga*
> ad togam Rūfī purpurandam *for purpling Rufus' toga*
> habēre togam *to have a toga*

**togās** *togas*
> togās purpurat *purples togas*
> volunt togās purpureās *they want purple togas*
> togās gerere *to wear togas*
> videt togās *sees togas*
> habēre togās *to have togas*

**Tyria** *Tyrian, from Tyre (i.e. Labanon), where sea snails for dyeing came from, and "Tyrian" can mean "purple" on its own*
> Poenica Tyria *Tyrian Poenica*
> nōn gerunt Tyria *don't wear Tyrian (i.e. purple) things*

habēre Tyria *to have Tyrian things*
**Tyriam** *Tyrian*
    volō habēre togam Tyriam *I want a Tyrian toga*
    togam Tyriam gerere *to wear a Tyrian toga*
**Tyriās** *Tyrian*
    volō togās Tyriās *I want Tyrian togas*
    togās Tyriās habēre *to have Tyrian togas*
**Tyriī** *Tyrian*
    mūricēs Tyriī *Tyrian sea snails*
    colōrēs Tyriī *Tyrian colors*
**Tyriōs** *Tyrian*
    habeō mūricēs Tyriōs multōs *I have many Tyrian sea snails*
**Tyrius** *Tyrian*
    sum Terrex Tyrius! *I'm Tyrian Terrex!*

# V

**valdē** *very, really*
**velle** *to want*
    ferunt 'Crixaflammam nōn velle...' *They say that*
                                 *Crixaflamma doesn't want*
**Vestālem** *Vestal, a sacred, highly honored priestess of Rome*
    Vestālem vidēre *to see the Vestal*
    vidētur esse Vestālem *it seems that it's a Vestal*
 **Vestālēs** *Vestals*
 **Vestālis** *Vestal*
**videō** *I see*
    nōn videō suffībula *I don't see any veils*
 **vidēre** *to see*
    nōn potest vidēre *isn't able to see*
    Sextum vidēre *to see Sextus*
    Rōmānum vidēre *to see the Roman*
    Vestālem vidēre *to see the Vestal*
 **vidēs** *you see*
    nōn vidēs Terregem Extraōrdinārium?! *You don't see*
                            *The Extraordinary Terrex?!*
**videt** *sees*
    videt multās togās *sees many togas*
    Poenicam videt *sees Poenica*
    videt fūnem *sees a rope*
    videt togās *sees togas*
    videt Oenobatiātum esse *sees that Oenobatiatus is*
    videt Crixaflammam *sees that Crixaflamma is*

**vidētur** *seems*
>> vidētur esse *it seems that it's*
>> vidētur Terregem esse *it seems that Terrex is*

**vīdit** *saw*
>> fūnem vīdit *saw a rope*

**vīs** *you want*
>> vīs esse fūnambula?! *You want to be a tightrope walker?!*
>> vīs togam pictam?! *You want a toga picta?!*

**vīsne?** *Do you want?*
>> vīsne esse? *Do you want to be?*
>> vīsne togam? *Do you want a toga?*

**vīvidae** *vivid (i.e. intensely clear, or bright)*
>> togae vīvidae *vivid togas*

**vīvidās** *vivid*
>> gerō togās vīvidās *I wear vivid togas*
>> habēs vīvidās togās Tyriās *you have vivid Tyrian togas*

**vīvidī** *vivid*
>> colōrēs vīvidī *vivid colors*

**vīvidissimī** *really vivid*
>> colōrēs vīvidissimī *really vivid colors*

**volō** *I want*
>> volō togam purpuream *I want a purple toga*
>> volō fūnambula esse *I want to be a tightrope walker*
>> volō attemptāre *I want to attempt*
>> volō purpurāre togam *I want to purple a toga*
>> volō togam purpurārī *I want the toga to be purpled*
>> volō habēre *I want to have*

**voluit** *wanted*
>> voluit togam praetextam *wanted a toga praetexta*

**volunt** *they want*
>> volunt togās purpureās *want purple togas*

**vult** *wants*
>> vult esse *wants to be*
>> vult ambulāre *wants to walk*
>> vult togam *wants a toga*
>> togam purpurārī vult *wants a toga to be purpled*
>> vult Poenicam purpurāre *wants Poenica to purple*
>> vult Crixaflammam esse *wants Crixaflamma to be*
>> vult persuādēre Oenobatiātō *wants to persuade Oenobatiatus*
>> vult Poenicam esse *wants Poenica to be*

**vultne?** *wants?*
>> vultne togam? *Does he want a toga?*

# Pisoverse Novellas & Resources

### Magister P's Pop-Up Grammar

*Pop-Up Grammar occurs when a student—not teacher—asks about a particular language feature, and the teacher offers a very brief explanation in order to continue communicating (i.e. interpreting, negotiating, and expressing meaning during reading or interacting).*

*Teachers can use this resource to provide such explanations, or students can keep this resource handy for reference when the teacher is unavailable. Characters and details from the Pisoverse novellas are used as examples of the most common of common Latin grammar.*

## Level AA
## Early Beginner

### Mārcus magulus
### (11 cognates + 8 other words)

*Marcus likes being a young Roman mage, but such a conspicuous combo presents problems in Egypt after he and his parents relocate from Rome. Despite generously offering his magical talents, this young mage feels like an obvious outsider, sometimes wishing he were invisible. Have you ever felt that way? Marcus searches Egypt for a place to be openly accepted, and even has a run-in with the famously fiendish Sphinx! Can Marcus escape unscathed?*

### Olianna et obiectum magicum
### (12 cognates + 12 other words)

*Olianna is different from the rest of her family, and finds herself excluded as a result. Have you ever felt that way? One day, a magical object appears that just might change everything for good. However, will it really be for the better? Can you spot any morals in this tale told from different perspectives?*

### Rūfus lutulentus
### (20 words)

*Was there a time when you or your younger siblings went through some kind of gross phase? Rufus is a Roman boy who likes to be muddy. He wants to be covered in mud everywhere in Rome, but quickly learns from Romans who bathe daily that it's not OK to do so in public. Can Rufus find a way to be muddy?*

## Rūfus et Lūcia: līberī lutulentī
## (25-70 words)

*Lucia, of Arianne Belzer's Lūcia: puella mala, joins Rufus in this collection of 18 additional stories. This muddy duo has fun in the second of each chapter expansion. Use to provide more exposure to words from the novella, or as a Free Voluntary Reading (FVR) option for all students, independent from Rūfus lutulentus.*

### Quīntus et nox horrifica
### (26 cognates, 26 other words)

*Monsters and ghosts...could they be real?! Is YOUR house haunted? Have YOU ever seen a ghost? Quintus is home alone when things start to go bump in the night in this scary novella. It works well with any Roman House unit, and would be a quick read for anyone interested in Pliny's ghost story.*

### Syra sōla
### (29 words)

*Syra likes being alone, but there are too many people everywhere in Rome! Taking her friend's advice, Syra travels to the famous coastal towns of Pompeii and Herculaneum in search of solitude. Can she find it?*

## Syra et animālia
## (35-85 words)

*In this collection of 20 additional stories, Syra encounters animals around Rome. Use to provide more exposure to words from the novella, or as a Free Voluntary Reading (FVR) option for all students, independent from Syra sōla.*

## Poenica purpurāria
## (16 cognates, 19 other words)

*Poenica is an immigrant from Tyre, the Phoenician city known for its purple. She's an extraordinary purple-dyer who wants to become a tightrope walker! In this tale, her shop is visited by different Romans looking to get togas purpled, as well as an honored Vestal in need of a new trim on her sacred veil. Some requests are realistic— others ridiculous. Is life all work and no play? Can Poenica find the time to tightrope walk?*

## Olianna et sandalia extraōrdināria
## (20 cognates, 20 other words)

*Olianna learns more about herself and her family in this psychological thriller continuation of "Olianna et obiectum magicum." We begin at a critical moment in the original, yet in this new tale, not only does the magical object appear to Olianna, but so do a pair of extraordinary sandals! Olianna has some choices to make. How will her decisions affect the timeline? Will things ever get back to normal? If so, is that for the better, or worse?*

## Pīsō perturbātus
## (36 words)

*Piso minds his Ps and Qs..(and Cs...and Ns and Os) in this alliterative tongue-twisting tale touching upon the Roman concepts of ōtium and negōtium. Before Piso becomes a little poet, early signs of an old curmudgeon can be seen.*

### Drūsilla in Subūrā
### (38 words)

*Drusilla is a Roman girl who loves to eat, but doesn't know how precious her favorite foods are. In this tale featuring all kinds of Romans living within, and beyond their means, will Drusilla discover how fortunate she is?*

### Rūfus et arma ātra
### (40 words)

*Rufus is a Roman boy who excitedly awaits an upcoming fight featuring the best gladiator, Crixaflamma. After a victorious gladiatorial combat in the Flavian Amphitheater (i.e. Colosseum), Crixaflamma's weapons suddenly go missing! Can Rufus help find the missing weapons?*

### Rūfus et gladiātōrēs
### (49-104 words)

*This collection of 28 stories adds details to characters and events from Rūfus et arma ātra, as well as additional, new cultural information about Rome, and gladiators. Use to provide more exposure to words from the novella, or as a Free Voluntary Reading (FVR) option for all students, independent from Rūfus et arma ātra.*

## *Level A*
## *Beginner*

### Mārcus et scytala Caesaris
### (20 cognates + 30 other words)

*Marcus has lost something valuable containing a secret message that once belonged to Julius Caesar. Even worse, it was passed down to Marcus' father for safekeeping, and he doesn't know it's missing! As Marcus and his friend Soeris search Alexandria for clues of its whereabouts, hieroglyphs keep appearing magically. Yet, are they to help, or hinder? Can Marcus decipher the hieroglyphs with Soeris' help, and find Caesar's secret message?*

## Agrippīna aurīga
## (24 cognates + 33 other words)

*Young Agrippina wants to race chariots, but a small girl from Lusitania couldn't possibly do that...could she?! After a victorious race in the stadium of Emerita, the local crowd favorite charioteer, Gaius Appuleius Dicloes, runs into trouble, and it's up to Agrippina to step into much bigger shoes. Can she take on the reins in this equine escapade?*

## diāria sīderum
## (30-60 cognates + 50-100 other words)

*Not much was known about The Architects— guardians of the stars—until their diaries were found in dark caves sometime in the Tenth Age. Explore their mysterious observations from the Seventh Age (after the Necessary Conflict), a time just before all evidence of their existence vanished for millenia! What happened to The Architects? Can you reconstruct the events that led to the disappearance of this ancient culture?*

## trēs amīcī et mōnstrum saevum
## (28 cognates + 59 other words)

*What became of the quest that Quintus' mother entrusted to Sextus and Syra in Drūsilla et convīvium magārum? Quintus finds himself alone in a dark wood (or so he thinks). Divine intervention is needed to keep Quintus safe, but can the gods overcome an ancient evil spurred on by Juno's wrath? How can Quintus' friends help?*

## sitne amor?
## (36 cognates, 53 other words)

*Piso and Syra are friends, but is it more than that? Sextus and his non-binary friend, Valens, help Piso understand his new feelings, how to express them, and how NOT to express them! This is a story of desire, and discovery. Could it be love?*

## ecce, poēmata discipulīs
## (77 cognates + 121 other words)

*"Wait, we have to read...Eutropius...who's that?! Homework on a Friday?! Class for an hour straight without a break?! Oh no, more tests in Math?! What, no glossary?! Why can't we just read?! Honestly, I was in bed (but the teacher doesn't know!)..." This collection of 33 poems is a humorous yet honest reflection of school, Latin class, homework, tests, Romans, teaching, and remote learning.*

## Magister P's Poetry Practice

*Ain't got rhythm? This book can help. You'll be presented with a rhythm and two words, phrases, or patterns, one of which matches. There are three levels, Noob, Confident, and Boss, with a total of 328 practice. This book draws its words, phrases, and patterns entirely from "ecce, poemata discipulis!," the book of poetry with over 270 lines of dactylic hexameter. Perhaps a first of its kind, too, this book can be used by students and their teacher at the same time. Therefore, consider this book a resource for going on a rhythmic journey together.*

## Agrippīna: māter fortis
## (65 words)

*Agrippīna is the mother of Rūfus and Pīsō. She wears dresses and prepares dinner like other Roman mothers, but she has a secret—she is strong, likes wearing armor, and can fight just like her husband! Can she keep this secret from her family and friends?*

## Līvia: māter ēloquens
## (44-86 words)

*Livia is the mother of Drusilla and Sextus. She wears dresses and prepares dinner like other Roman mothers, but she has a secret—she is well-spoken, likes wearing togas, and practices public speaking just like her brother, Gaius! Can she keep this secret from her family and friends? Livia: mater eloquens includes 3 versions under one cover. The first level, (Alpha), is simpler than Agrippina: mater fortis; the second level, (Beta) is the same level, and the third, (Gamma-Delta) is more complex.*

### Pīsō et Syra et pōtiōnēs mysticae
### (163 cognates, 7 other words)

*Piso can't seem to write any poetry. He's distracted, and can't sleep. What's going on?! Is he sick?! Is it anxiety?! On Syra's advice, Piso seeks mystical remedies that have very—different—effects. Can he persevere?*

### Drūsilla et convīvium magārum
### (58 words)

*Drusilla lives next to Piso. Like many Romans, she likes to eat, especially peacocks! As the Roman army returns, she awaits a big dinner party celebrating the return of her father, Julius. One day, however, she sees a suspicious figure give something to her brother. Who was it? Is her brother in danger? Is she in danger?*

# Level B
# Advanced Beginner

### mȳthos malus: convīvium Terregis
### (41 cognates + 56 other words)

*An obvious nod to Petronius' Cena Trimalchionis, yes, but this is not an adaptation, by any means. In this tale, Terrex can't get anything right during his latest dinner party. He's confused about Catullus' carmina, and says silly things left and right as his guests do all they can to be polite, though patience is running low. With guests even fact-checking amongst themselves, can Terrex say something remotely close to being true? Will the guests mind their manners and escape without offending their host?*

## sīgna zōdiaca Vol. 1
**(63 cognates, 84 other words)**
## sīgna zōdiaca Vol. 2
**(63 cognates, 92 other words)**
## sīgna zōdiaca Vol. 3
**(62 cognates, 93 other words)**

*Do you like stories about gods and monsters? Did you know that the zodiac signs are based on Greek and Roman mythology? Your zodiac sign can tell you a lot about yourself, but not everyone feels that strong connection. Are your qualities different from your sign? Are they the same? Read signa zodiaca to find out! These readers are part non-fiction, and part Classical adaptation, providing information about the zodiac signs as well as two tiered versions of associated myths.*

# Level C
# Low Intermediate

### fragmenta Pīsōnis
### (96 words)

*This collection of poetry is inspired by scenes and characters from the Pisoverse, and features 50 new lines of poetry in dactylic hexameter, hendecasyllables, and scazon (i.e. limping iambics)! fragmenta Pīsōnis can be used as a transition to the Piso Ille Poetulus novella, or as additional reading for students comfortable with poetry having read the novella already.*

### Pīsō Ille Poētulus
### (108 words)

*Piso is a Roman boy who wants to be a great poet like Virgil. His family, however, wants him to be a soldier like his father. Can Piso convince his family that poetry is a worthwhile profession? Features 22 original, new lines of dactylic hexameter.*

### Pīsō: Tiered Versions
### (68-138 words)

*This novella combines features of Livia: mater eloquens with the tiered versions of the Piso Ille Poetulus story taken from its Teacher's Guide and Student Workbook. There are 4 different levels under one cover, which readers choose, switching between them at any time. Piso: Tiered Versions could be used as scaffolding for reading the original novella, Piso Ille Poetulus. Alternatively, it could be read independently as a Free Voluntary Reading (FVR) option, leaving it up to the learner which level to read.*

### Tiberius et Gallisēna ultima
### (155 words)

*Tiberius is on the run. Fleeing from an attacking Germanic tribe, the soldier finds himself separated from the Roman army. Trying to escape Gaul, he gets help from an unexpected source—a magical druid priestess (a "Gaul" in his language, "Celt" in hers). With her help, can Tiberius survive the punishing landscape of Gaul with the Germanic tribe in pursuit, and make his way home to see Rufus, Piso, and Agrippina once again?*

# ...and more!
*See magisterp.com for the latest:*

*teacher's materials
other books
audio*

Made in the USA
Columbia, SC
30 August 2022